MW00564684

Arlene Holden

ENCOURAGE YOURSELF

SHORT STORIES TO
EMPOWER YOUR DAY

Arlene Holden

𝕻𝖊𝖆𝖗𝖑𝖞 𝕲𝖆𝖙𝖊𝖘 𝕻𝖚𝖇𝖑𝖎𝖘𝖍𝖎𝖓𝖌 𝕷𝕷𝕮
INSPIRING CHRISTIAN AUTHORS TO BE AUTHORS

Pearly Gates Publishing, LLC, Harlem, Georgia (USA)

Encourage Yourself:
Short Stories to Empower Your Day

Copyright © 2022
Arlene Holden

Print ISBN 13: 978-1-948853-59-0
Digital ISBN 13: 978-1-948853-60-6
Library of Congress Control Number: 2022920883

Scripture references are taken from the King James Version (KJV) of the Holy Bible and used with permission from Zondervan via Biblegateway.com
Public Domain.

Pearly Gates Publishing, LLC
Angela Edwards, CEO
P.O. Box 639
Harlem, GA 30814
BestSeller@PearlyGatesPublishing.com

v

DEDICATION AND ACKNOWLEDGEMENTS

This book is dedicated to my three children,
Steven,
Florence,
And
Joanna,
their families and my siblings.

Many thanks to those who prayed for me
during the days of preparation.

To God be the glory,
for He has done great things—
wherein I am glad!

CORE SCRIPTURE

"I CAN DO ALL THINGS THROUGH CHRIST WHICH STRENGTHENETH ME."
PHILIPPIANS 4:13

TABLE OF CONTENTS

MY EARLY EXISTENCE

The date was September 11, 1939. At the time, my parents lived in Bridgeton, New Jersey, in the township of Stow Creek. It was a warm summer day, and the time had come for James and Pearl's third child—**me**—to be born.

I will share with you the story that was told to me...

There was no telephone service in the home, so my mother's sister walked approximately half a mile to call the doctor to tell him my mother was in labor.

"How far apart are the pains?" he asked, prompting my aunt to take that half-mile walk back to my parents. Once she received the answer, she walked *back* to the telephone to give the doctor the message. Because babies were born at home those days, he needed to know how soon it would be before I would be born so that he had enough time to arrive to help deliver me. What a tiresome day that had to be for my aunt with all of that back and forth. Still, my mother had the biggest job ahead of her: birthing me.

1

One of my mother's cousins named me Arlene, after her mother-in-law. Out of the children my mother had, I was the smallest baby. She said they carried me on a pillow for a while because they were afraid to hold me.

We did not have an electric or gas range for cooking or heating. Instead, we used wood, coal, or kerosene. The wallpaper would become discolored from the smoke and fumes emitted from the stoves.

Although our family didn't have much money, when a baby was born, everything had to be just as right as my mother could make it. For example, before the baby was born, wallpapering and painting were done (if needed), and toiletries were purchased. Those necessities included:

- Johnson's baby oil
- Lotion
- Cream
- Palmolive and Ivory soaps
- Absorbent cotton to dip in a boric acid solution to cleanse the newborn's eyes, nose, and mouth

There was also a lot of fuss about the laundry. Brand-new diapers were washed in Ivory Snow powder or Ivory flakes. Mom said, "The newness must be washed out of the diapers to be made soft for the baby's skin." She never took the cloth diapers directly out of the package and put them on her baby. She always washed them first. On a sunshiny day, seeing the clothesline full of baby clothes flopping in the wind was a beautiful sight, and the scent of spring rain added delight to those moments in time.

You might wonder why I said "diapers" and not "pampers." In those days, there were no pampers. As a matter of fact, no one even heard of them. The diaper laundry service was an option for those who could afford it—but that's not my story. It seemed that God always provided whatever my mother needed for her babies.

As time passed, my mother said I began to walk (as toddlers do), but then I stopped walking for no apparent reason. My paternal grandfather thought it happened because of his polio. I was told he would hold me on his lap and bathe my legs with white potato water to get me moving again. (I suppose potato water was one of those old remedies used for conditions such as what I had.) I do not

3

know how long I stopped walking or if the potato water had anything to do with my healing, but I praise God for His healing power!

Around 1942, during World War II, my parents relocated our family to Rosenhayn, New Jersey, in the township of Deerfield. I was around three years old and can recall the blackouts and air raids. At night, we heard warplanes flying low over our home. I remember the times the lights inside our home were turned off, and we would sit in total darkness. My mother's sister-in-law would try to finish some chores from the light of the moon that shined through a window. The lights that typically illuminated the streets were also dark, and a constable or police officer walked the streets, ensuring every residence obeyed the "Lights-Out" law.

As I grew older, I recall tagging along with my older siblings and cousins when they went to the circus at a local synagogue. Twenty-five cents went a long way in those days. We rode the swings, ponies, and merry-go-round. We ate popcorn, cotton candy, and hot dogs and drank soda pop. What a fun day! I also remember playing with mom's hand-winding Victrola turntable that played number 78 records, as well as times when I had fun playing with her pretty lilac high-heel shoes...pretending I was a lady.

There was a door between the kitchen and dining room that "helped" to pull our loose teeth. Our father would tie one end of a string around the loose tooth and the other end to the doorknob. He would instruct us to walk away from the door. Other times, the door would be shut in a hurry. You guessed correctly if you said, "And that tooth popped right out!" Nowadays, I imagine pulling teeth in that way might be considered child abuse, but in those days, parents did what they knew to do to get the job done. According to the Holy Bible, we are only held accountable for what we know (see 1 Timothy 1:13). God is merciful!

Our family was rapidly growing. I was the third child, had a younger brother, and my mom was expecting her fifth child. One day, my maternal grandparents visited our home and requested that I go and live with them. Grandmom said that I would be company and a help to her. In those days, money was hard to come by, so it was probably easy for my parents to say yes to her request. I imagine my mother being hesitant to agree to the arrangement, but she respected her parents and always wanted to please them. Before I knew it, I was all packed up, and away I went to the farm to be introduced to the chickens, pigs, dogs, and cats. There was also a rooster that chased me, horses, fresh fruits and vegetables, and (when I became old enough) plenty of hard work.

Although I was lonely, that feeling didn't last long. I was given toys, treats, money, and plenty of one-on-one attention. I played house, church, and school with my doll and paper dolls. Sadly, doing those things is something many small children of today do not know anything about. I also had a swing set. Many times, I would swing so high I wished I could reach the sky.

I was fortunate to have many things to occupy my mind back in those days to keep me busy. Even today—at age 83—I can still find things at home to do that keep me busy.

Sometimes, we must encourage ourselves through the Word of God! (Read Philippians 4:8)

ENCOURAGE YOURSELF

"Why art thou cast down, O my soul? And why art thou disquieted within me? Hope thou in God; for I shall yet praise Him, who is the health of my countenance, and my God."
Psalm 42:11

W e have a decision to make: Do we remain discouraged, or do we believe in God and have victory when facing adversities?

Trials and adversities often discourage us, but they also help mature us into whom God would have us to be. Yes, many discouragements have been painful, but they are necessary.

After experiencing several tests, I thank God that I know for myself that trials and trusting Him to bring me out have given me more strength to climb the mountains before me. God helped me to encourage myself. However, what worked for me may not work for you—but it's worth a try if you feel that all else has failed. It is good to look beyond our surroundings, dreams, and hope and see the gifts and blessings from God.

7

"Now, faith is the substance of things hoped for, the evidence of things not seen."
Hebrews 11:1

Hebrews 13:5c says, "...for He hath said, 'I will never leave thee, nor forsake thee'"—but there's something we must do first. David makes it plain: "I will bless the Lord at all times; His praise shall continually be in my mouth" (Psalm 34:1).

In every life, some rain must fall. After the rain, the sun will shine again, but our faith will be tested time and again.

"Man that is born of a woman is of a few days and full of trouble."
Job 14:1

I would like to think that no one wants to be sick, everyone would have enough money to meet their needs, and no one would feel lonely and deserted—as if nobody loves nor cares about them.

We serve a great God who is concerned about us, regardless of what it looks like. He waits with outstretched arms to protect us from the storms of life. When we sometimes fail to trust Him, He doesn't give up on us.

"God so loved the world that He gave His only begotten Son, that whosoever believes in Him shall not perish, but have everlasting life."
John 3:16

The Bible tells us about Job—a rich, perfect, upright man who feared God. The Bible also says that one day, the sons of God came to present themselves to the Lord, and Satan came among them. God asked Satan, "Where did you come from?" Satan replied, "From going to and fro in the earth, and from walking up and down in it." (Job 1:6-7)

Satan told God that Job walked upright because God had increased Job's substance. God allowed Satan to afflict Job's body and destroy all of his children and possessions. Why would God allow such a thing? Because He knew Job loved Him and would not lose his integrity. Job knew in whom he believed. He knew God would never leave nor forsake him.

When Job's wife turned her back on him and said, "Dost thou still retain thine integrity? Curse God and die," Job told her she spoke like a foolish woman. He then said,

9

"If a man die, shall he live again? All the days of my appointed time, I will wait till my change comes." (Job 14:14)

Job withstood the test and encouraged himself, even amid the distraught state he was in and all while his body was covered with boils from the crown of his head to the soles of his feet.

"So, the Lord blessed the latter end of Job more than his beginning."
Job 42:12a

When I was young, I enjoyed reading love stories. What I read led me to believe that was how life was supposed to be (glamorous, money to buy everything I needed, and lots of love). Well, my family didn't have a lot of money, but it seemed I always had what I needed the most (food, clothing, and shelter). Holidays were happy days, and I anticipated days to celebrate something special every month of the year. It seemed overall, people were happier and easier to get along with in those days, especially those I would meet while shopping for the Thanksgiving and Christmas holidays.

There's a song that says, "There is no secret what God can do. What He's done for others, He can do for you!" With God's help, I encouraged and lifted myself out of that "left alone" and "I do not understand" mood. I am not ashamed to say I was my own psychologist. The therapy cost me nothing because I trusted God. I label it a God-given gift.

Monthly Healing On My Christian Journey

I started my "therapy" in January. It was the beginning of a new year and a time to "forget those things behind and reach forth unto those things which are before." I chose that month to look for a better life with new hopes and dreams.

February is Heart Month—the Love Month. Valentine's Day is celebrated as "The Lovers' Holiday." Jesus told the disciples, "Love ye one another..." (John 15:12). Again, I looked for new beginnings. I visualized caring, sharing, loving, and exchanging kind words and tenderness.

The expectation of hope and better days gave me strength for the days to come and carried me into the month of March. "A soft answer turns away wrath: but grievous words stir up anger" (Proverbs 15:1). I got married in March and had high hopes as I awaited our wedding anniversary. I looked back to what I thought were the happiest days and looked forward to a fresh start.

Easter typically falls in April, and there were special events at the church. Sewing was one of my hobbies, so I made my daughter's Easter outfits.

The days were getting warmer, buds and flowers ushered in the month of May, and the promise of spring was in the air. When I lived in my mobile home, I had planted flowers and prepared the yard for spring by the time Mother's Day came.

June was the month of opportunities, step-ups, and graduations. I looked forward to summertime when life was easier and the children would be on summer break. The grass was greener, and there were signs of new life and new hope. The birds tweeted their songs in the morning, the bumble bees flew around trying to extract nectar from the blooming flowers, and before I knew it, July arrived. Where did the time go?

In July, we celebrated Independence Day on the fourth. We would have a cookout and watch the fireworks at night. I remember the County Fair being in July as well.

The month of August kept me busy. There were many birthdays that month, and I had to prepare the children for school in September. August was also the month we had our church's annual picnic.

September was another busy month. We celebrated my birthday, Labor Day (the last summer holiday), and the return of children to school. The cool September mornings paved the way for October.

I loved seeing the beautiful landscape when the leaves turned yellow, orange, red, and purple, sometimes mixed with green ones that hadn't changed color. With the scorching summer months in the north a thing of the past, we welcomed the early frost on the pumpkins. October is also sweater and jacket weather.

Every day should be a day of thanksgiving. God has given us so much, but most importantly, He gave His only begotten Son, who died on Calvary's Cross for the sins of the world. We do not have to live in shame anymore. We can accept Jesus as Savior and Lord of our lives (read Romans 10:9-13). In November, I looked forward to preparing Thanksgiving dinner along with pies, cakes, family gatherings, and such. God always provided and made a way. Therefore, I am forever grateful.

Jesus brought love and joy to the world! The month of December is so special and always busy. We celebrate Jesus' birth, sing Christmas carols, participate in church activities, address cards, shop for loved ones, and say "Merry Christmas" to strangers.

When I think of the traditional Christmas colors—white, red, and green—this is what I feel:

- White represents God's holiness and righteousness.
- Red represents the blood that Jesus shed so that we might be saved.

- Green represents life. God is from everlasting to everlasting, and He sent His Son to give everlasting life to all who will believe and do His will.

For whatever reason, that "therapy" was the way I maintained my relationship with the Lord and functioned in what seemed to be an upside-down world.

There are people who have special needs in the natural and those who have special spiritual needs. I was the latter, but Jesus loved me, held onto me, and led me to the church—even when I didn't feel like going. One of my pastors told the members of his church to be faithful and attend church, even when we didn't feel like it. I recall him saying, "Even if you do not have an offering and transportation is available, come to church anyway. God will bless you for your faithfulness. Do what the Bible says, even when unsure why you are doing what you do. God knows your heart. He is in control."

I wish that in my earlier years of walking with the Lord, I knew how to really let go and let God have control of my life. I suppose it's better late than never. When we accept Jesus as our Savior, there is so much growing that must be done, just like in the natural. My pastor taught me to be steadfast in prayer and the things of God by reading my Bible, allowing the words to become a part of me. He urged remaining close to the family of God and do whatever my hands find to do in Kingdom building. I feel I have come through valleys and trudged rough ground but know in whom I believe today. I made it to the main highway and found the answer. Along the way, I learned to pray with faith and allow it to guide me. I am "looking for that blessed hope, and the glorious appearing of our Lord and Savior Jesus Christ" (Titus 2:13).

We won't always get a pat on the back from people and told we are doing a good job, but we can encourage ourselves. Sometimes, we have to do it—no matter what it looks like. Don't be defeated by the enemy. "The thief comes not but for to steal, and to kill, and to destroy; I am come that they might have life, and that they might have it more abundantly" (John 10:10). If I can help somebody along the way, my living will not be in vain.

God Bless you! Jesus loves you!

MY TESTIMONY

"I will bless the LORD at all times; His praise shall continually be in my mouth."
Psalm 34:1

When I reflect on my life and think things over, I can truly say I have been blessed. I have a testimony! God was making a way for me when I was unaware. From the time I can remember, I was taught that God lived in Heaven and that if I were a good girl, I would live with Him forever when I die. Conversely, I would go to Hell and live with the devil forever if I was bad. I didn't want to go to Hell, so I always tried to be good—especially when I was around my grandparents, at school, around other adults, and with my sisters and brothers. If one of my siblings saw me do something wrong, they would say, "I'm going to tell mom," or "I'm going to tell Mom-Mom." I didn't want the whipping that was sure to follow (yes, children got whippings in those days).

As I got older, I heard my grandfather and preacher say I needed to be saved. Getting saved looked hard to me. Satan doesn't want any of us to be saved, so why wouldn't

17

he make accepting Jesus as Savior and Lord of my life appear hard? God watched over and protected me through the years. I give Him all honor, praise, and glory, for they belong to Him!

When I was 16, I went on a boat ride with my older siblings and some others. I remember the day as if it were yesterday. No one in the group professed salvation, and some of the guys were drinking. As the boat began to leave the dock, we noticed the water was coming on board. They tried to bail it out with beer cans, but the water was coming on board too fast. Someone finally got some sense and decided we needed to return to shore. As soon as my sister and I stepped off the boat, it sank. Neither my sister nor I could swim, and our brother knew how to swim to the point of saving himself. Look at God! I thank Him for His love, His grace, and His mercy.

The story's point is this: God stepped in right on time. If I had drowned that day, I would have been lost forever—lifting my eyes toward Heaven from Hell. God's Word is true. He means what He says. "Therefore, be ye also ready…" (Matthew 24:44).

"The Lord appeared unto Abram, and said unto him, 'I am the Almighty God; walk before Me, and be thou perfect.'"
Genesis 17:1b

God has not changed. What He says to one, He says to all.

"Sanctify yourselves, therefore, and be ye holy: for I am the Lord your God."
Leviticus 20:7

"And ye shall be holy unto Me: for I the Lord am holy, and have severed you from other people, that ye should be Mine."
Leviticus 20:26

In my younger days, I went to dances and tried to be one of the best-dressed people at the affair. If I only knew then what I know now, I would have served God a long time ago. I now realize how important it is for everyone to have a relationship with Jesus while they are young. If I had only applied the Word of God to my life sooner and not leaned on my own understanding, I would have avoided a lot of heartaches.

"Trust in the Lord with all thine heart; and lean not unto thine own understanding."
Proverbs 3:5

For a time, the following described me:

"Traitors, heady, high-minded, lovers of pleasure more than lovers of God..."
2 Timothy 3:4

My grandparents told me the "Do's and Don'ts," but I could not live what the scriptures said because I was not saved. I had not accepted Jesus as my Savior. Jesus tells us, "...without Me, ye can do nothing" (John 15:5d).

I recall the time I was hurrying to get ready for a party. I paused for a moment and asked myself, "Why am I rushing?" The response came from an inner voice:

"You know that you are not saved yet."

I do not proudly say this, but I continued to get ready for the party. God was talking, but I wasn't listening.

"Today, if you hear His voice, harden not your heart."
Psalm 95:7c-8

When I was a child, it was mandatory that children went to church. The saints were reaching out to lost souls, praying they would become convicted and accept Jesus as their Savior and Lord. Some of the soul-searching songs that were sung during altar call included:

- "You Must Be Born Again"
- "Come to Jesus"
- "Don't Let it Be Said, 'Too Late to Enter the Golden Gate'"
- "Throw Out the Lifeline" and
- "If Thou Be Saved, Why Not Tonight?"

Those songs made you feel like crawling under the bench!

When I began my Christian journey at the age of 23, it was hard for me to believe that all I had to do was be sorry for the sins I had committed and believe. I did not know how to talk to God—the one I could not see. I was trained to be seen and heard, mostly when asked questions or when playing outside.

"That if thou shalt confess with thy mouth the Lord Jesus, and shalt believe in thine heart that God hath raised Him from the dead, thou shalt be saved. For with the heart, man believes unto righteousness; and with the mouth, confession is made unto salvation. For the scripture saith, 'Whosoever believes in Him shall not be

ashamed.' For there is no difference between the Jew and the Greek: for the same Lord over all is rich unto all that call upon Him. For whosoever shall call upon the name of the Lord shall be saved."
Romans 10:9-13

I really didn't know how to believe in and trust God, but this I did know: I did not want to go to Hell. I asked Jesus to save me and was told I would become sanctified by refraining from the things of the world; I was now a new creature in Christ Jesus. On my new journey, I became twisted in my thoughts, but I thank God for a praying mother, a concerned pastor, and the pastor's wife. I felt my prayers were going nowhere. When I stopped attending church for a few Sundays, the Lord showed up one day and told me I should not be sitting home on a Sunday morning watching television and playing games. I should've been in church.

That day, I listened to those wandering thoughts. I got myself and my children together and returned to the church. That morning, the pastor's message was, "There is Nothing Too Hard for God." My faith increased, and I returned to church for the evening service. The sermon's topic was a continuation of the morning service: "If There Is Nothing Too Hard for God, Why Don't You Trust Him?"

I am so grateful that God has been so patient with me. It is not His will that any of us should perish.

"For God so loved the world, that He gave His only begotten Son, that whosoever believes in Him shall not perish but have everlasting life."
John 3:16

I may not have understood then, but I thank God that I understand now. God is an Awesome God! He is able to do all that He has promised He would do. Truly, there is none like Him. God is able to do all things but fail. He brought me out of the darkness into the marvelous light. God opened my eyes so that I may see to follow Him.

God gave me the strength to raise my children when times were hard. My husband was not saved, and the Bible says, "Can two walk together except they be agreed?" It seemed we had more negative days than positive ones. I desired to work but had no transportation. God made a way for me to do domestic work. The ladies I worked for came to my home in their car and took me to their home to do a day's work. While I was on my hands and knees scrubbing floors, I asked God for a better job. A prominent lady in our township asked me if I would be interested in driving a school bus. At first, I thought, "Me? Driving a school bus?" I was so happy, though! God had heard my prayer and gotten me off my knees from scrubbing floors.

I learned how to drive the bus and then went to the Motor Vehicle Division for testing. I passed and was on my way to better things in life! Thank You, Jesus! I was allowed to keep the bus parked at my home. Therefore, I could stop at the country store and post office before picking up the children or after I had completed my run.

God has a way of opening doors that seem to be closed. The adversary does not want us to feel free and be happy; he wants us to be weighed down with the cares of this life. Since the Lord delivered me, why should I be bound?

As time passed, God gave me the mind and ability to attend night school to get my GED. (It's never too late to return to school and achieve.) I also attended a Licensed Practical Nurse Program and graduated in March of 1978.

God has done so much for me that I cannot tell it all. The most important thing He did was look beyond my faults and see that I was in need of a Savior. God is my refuge and strength, a very present help in trouble. God is a rock in a weary land and a shelter in the time of storm. He is the lifter of my head.

The enemy is mad at all who have a relationship with the Lord and does not care how he interrupts God's plan. My grandfather used to sing a song that said, "Just a closer walk with Thee; grant it, Jesus, is my plea; daily walking close to Thee; let it be, Dear Lord, let it be." To be under God's protective care plan, we must walk very close to Him.

About 50 years ago, I went through a period of depression. It is a long story, but in short, God brought me out. Satan tried to make me end my life. It was hard for me to deal with life at the time and try to face people in my condition. The enemy had it all planned out. I could either wander in the woods and eventually die from lack of nutrition, or I could hitch a ride with just anyone, go to another town, and start over. All the while, the enemy was trying to make me lose my mind!

I thank God for the love that He showed toward me. He reminded me of His Holy Word. I couldn't wander in the woods and die because the Bible says, "Thou shalt not kill." I could not run away because I would've abandoned my family. The Bible says, "Let not your good be evil spoken of" (Romans 14:16). Also, if there had been an accident while I was riding in a car with strangers, it would have been very easy for people to think I had been unfaithful.

It seemed all motivation to proceed with the enemy's plan was gone. Instead, I went through the motions of doing things for my family. When I told my mother how I felt, she prayed with me. When I prayed in my alone time, I made my altar anywhere feasible. I thank God for my pastor and his wife during that time in my life. The pastor's wife said, "If you do not have any faith, believe God and go on my faith." Wow! She sounded just like a mother!

One day, while at home alone, I looked at a picture of my eldest daughter. She had a pretty, little grin with her tooth coming in. As I looked at the photo, I smiled. I knew at that moment I had been delivered! God had heard and answered my prayer! It may not seem like much to you, but when you have felt you were void of emotions and then smile, it's miraculous! I began to give God glory, honor, and praise! I felt like climbing the highest building I could think of (the Empire State Building came to mind) and telling the world I was free! To God be the glory for all He has done!

About 40 years ago, I woke up with pain in my right hip—one that seemed to warrant a physician's assessment. As I turned the pages of the telephone book, seeking the least expensive alternative (primary care or orthopedic doctor), the following words pushed their way through my cluttered train of thoughts: "And with His stripes, we are healed" (Isaiah 53:5d). I began to repeat those words over and over. My faith increased to the point I didn't call the doctor. Instead, I climbed back into bed and thanked God for His healing power. To this day, I have not had any more issues in that area, except for when I have exercised too much. Look at God! Won't He do it?

The Flesh Attack

When I was 16, I had problems with my skin. My mother thought it might have come from working on my grandfather's farm. I was seen and treated by a dermatologist and thought I was healed.

As a Nurse's Aide, I washed my hands frequently. They became very dry, causing an itchy rash. Medicated topical creams provided much relief.

In 2007, my skin was attacked again. I had been working in my yard, preparing things for Mother's Day. One evening, as I prepared for bed, I saw a tiny red ball on my abdomen that resembled a small ball of blood. I just knew it was a tick. I tried to pull it off by pinching it between my fingers but could not. Neither rubbing alcohol nor Vaseline worked either. I then grabbed a pair of pliers to do the job. The more I attempted to remove it, the more some (or maybe all) of the blood retreated to under my skin. When I finally got it off, I observed its brown, round, and flat shape. I cleaned the area, covered it, and treated it until it healed...or so I thought. One day, I noticed it had eviscerated. I should have gone to the doctor immediately, but I didn't. As a matter of fact, I should have gone to the emergency room when I first discovered the tiny red ball, but I didn't because I thought I could handle it.

Then there was the time I was invited to go on vacation to Canada. In the hotel room where I stayed, I hit my shin three times on a metal piece on the bottom of the bed frame. The last time I hit my shin, it felt like a horse had kicked me! The skin broke, the area began to swell, and a hematoma formed. The hotel did not have a first-aid kit, so the Registered Nurse in our group applied ice and instructed me to keep my leg elevated. I didn't think to have someone go to a drugstore in Canada to purchase an over-the-counter antibiotic. Instead, I waited until returning to New Jersey. Once home, I went to the hospital to get an x-ray to rule out a fracture and then visited the primary doctor to get a tetanus shot. I was also seen and treated by my podiatrist. Healing was a slow process.

There was also the time I broke out in hives, which meant visiting the dermatologist when over-the-counter medication didn't resolve the problem. Throughout that summer, I went from doctor to doctor, trying to find some answers and relief. Orders were given for special soaps, lotions, etc., but I continued to break out with different sizes, shapes, and colors of pimples or rashes. I had lesions almost everywhere on my body except my face. The first week in September, I went to the University of Penn ER. That was where the first biopsies and cultures were done. By then, my nerves were edgy. I had grown weak, the lesions were draining more, and my appetite was not good.

I thought I was dying a slow death and started to write my will.

I was seen by a dermatologist at the University of Penn by appointment from September 1, 2007, until the last day of February 2008. During that time, I was seen and evaluated by approximately 21 dermatologists from all over the world. None came up with a diagnosis of my condition. I never knew if the skin condition resulted from the suspected tick bite or from germs entering my bloodstream when I injured my shin while in Canada. Perhaps it was none of the above...

In the latter part of September, the dermatologist prescribed Prednisone (30 mg.) daily, which was titrated to 2 mg. daily. The last dosage taken was in January 2008. It was a long journey, and I appreciate the doctors who tried to help. Most importantly, I thank God for Jesus. He is my Ultimate Healer, my Provider, my Everything! Although I only shared half of the story, to God be the glory! I am glad I knew who Jesus was before I was attacked. By faith, I began thanking God for healing me before I saw any results.

One morning in October 2008, I fainted. I do not know why, but I wasn't afraid because I knew God was with me. It was very painful but also very necessary. I thank God for the friends who loved me unconditionally and did not kick me to the curb when I was down. They are true friends. I also thank God for my oldest sister, who came to see about me and helped me out, as well as for those who prayed for me. The Bible says we are to bear one another's burdens (see Galatians 6:2).

I am so grateful for God's healing power and even more thankful for His saving grace. I am not perfect (none of us are), but it was the shed blood of Jesus that made me whole. His love lifted me when I had no strength or power of my own. Jesus loves unconditionally. He will never leave you, nor will He forsake you. He will be there in the midnight hour. He will wipe the tears away and turn your midnight into day. He can mend your broken heart and fill the void in all situations. He is my Rose of Sharon and my Bright and Morning Star. He is a wheel in the middle of a wheel. He is the Great I Am. Our Heavenly Father will be everything that we need Him to be.

I serve a Mighty God... an Omnipotent God...a Loving God...a Merciful God. My hope is built on nothing less than Jesus' blood and righteousness. I dare not trust the sweetest frame, but wholly lean on Jesus' name. I hope in the Lord because it is through His mercies that I am not consumed. His compassions, they fail not and are new every morning. Great is God's faithfulness!

I am frail, and my life is but a vapor, but when I talk about the Lord, He makes me feel like I am a giant! I have learned to bless God's name when things are going well and not so well because He deserves total praise.

I cannot tell it all, but I pray my testimony has encouraged someone.

You can make it. Jesus' blood has never lost its power. He is still making a way for me, and He will always make a way for you! Whatever you may be going through, "look to God: He is the author and the finisher of your faith" (Hebrews 12:2).

COME TO JESUS

"In times like these, we need a Savior. In times like these, we need an anchor. Be very sure your anchor holds and grips a solid rock, and that Rock is Jesus." (Ruth C. Jones)

I t would have been so beneficial for me if I could have trusted Jesus to be my Rock when I was a teenager. I didn't know Him as my Refuge and Strength, a very present help in trouble. Today I know that Jesus is dependable, strong, and everything we need.

I was reared in a Christian home by my grandparents. We attended church religiously—almost every Sunday. There were times we went to church every night except Saturday (I imagine that was during revival week). The older saints were looking for Jesus to return every day of the week. God has not changed. We should also be looking, watching, and waiting for Jesus' return.

"Therefore, be ye also ready; for in such an hour as ye think not, the Son of Man will come."
Matthew 24:44

Before the COVID-19 pandemic, many revivals were held, but the crisis has changed how we fellowship.

Regardless, it does not prevent us from praying and making an altar anywhere. We do not need a lot of space to pray to Jesus.

The first spiritual lessons I learned as a child were to be a good girl (behave myself) so that I would go to Heaven when I die. I had to say my prayers before going to bed, speak the truth, and don't lie, cheat, or steal.

The first Bible scripture I learned was John 3:16: "For God so loved the world, He gave His only Begotten Son; that whosoever believes in Him shall not perish but have everlasting life."

When we went to church on Sunday, we sometimes attended several services in one day: Sunday school, morning service, afternoon service, youth program, and night service. Each service seemed long...and they were. There was praying, singing, shouting (dancing in the Spirit), testimonies, preaching, and the invitation to come to Jesus and be saved. Even though the service may have lasted all day, the evening preacher often didn't stand to preach until 10:00 p.m.—and he would preach for about an hour. Time was not a factor in those days. People were panting after God like the hart [deer] panted after the water brook; so panted their souls after God (read Psalm 42:1).

When the altar call was made for sinners to be saved, I should have been one of those seeking salvation. I felt that I was young and certainly didn't think I wanted to live like what I saw in the elders. I thought Jesus was only for older people, but I was wrong. I didn't understand the love of Jesus and that I needed a relationship with Him more than anything else in the world. We can go to Heaven with a sick body, but we cannot go to Heaven with a sin-sick soul. We must be born again (see John 3:3).

Since becoming older in the faith, I see the importance of mothers praying for their babies while they are yet in the womb. There are some nursery rhymes our little ones do not need to know. Thank God for the authors who still write Bible stories for children. Family prayer time before the family goes their separate ways during the day (to work, school, etc.) and before retiring to bed is needful. The Bible says, "Train up a child in the way he should go; and when he is old, he will not depart from it" (Proverbs 22:6).

When I was in grammar school, some of us students huddled together during recess and sang songs from a Hit Parade book brought in by one of the girls who "knew more" than most of us. (It was against school regulations to huddle in such a way.) The enemy has continued to try to set traps for God's creation of humankind since the fall of Adam and Eve in the Garden of Eden.

"And the serpent said unto the woman,
'Ye shall not surely die.'"
Genesis 3:4

The traps set for me were love songs at school and love stories at home. To this day, I cannot believe my grandmother let me get away with reading those books. I likely hid them (I honestly cannot remember), but I know now that what I did wasn't right. It may seem like a little thing, but the Song of Solomon 2:15b says, "...the little foxes destroy the vine, for our vines have tender grapes."

To the best of my grandparents' knowledge and their relationship with the Lord, they tried to show me the ways of the Lord, but Satan was on his job, luring me into the things of the world. Since I had not accepted Jesus as my Savior and Lord, it was very easy to be enticed by worldly things. Years ago, most children were not bold with their wrongdoings as some children are today. Still, that did not make the sins that we committed right. God saw everything we did. Sin is sin, regardless of who it is in.

I do not proudly say that while sitting in English class, I remember doodling and daydreaming about being on a cruise ship, dressed in a gown, with my imaginary companion dressed in a tuxedo. I imagined him removing his coat to place it around my shoulders because of the coolness of the night air as the ship moved across the water. Everyone needs to be loved, but I believe some of my daydreaming about love came from exposure to love stories and singing songs from the Hit Parade books.

In the natural, it is said that we are what we eat. If we eat the wrong kinds of food, we may get sick or gain/lose weight. If we feed our spirit junk, that is what we become by consuming empty calories with no spiritual power.

I feel the need to speak those things into your life because it is essential to have a relationship with Jesus at an early age to help lead and guide us through life. Not knowing Jesus is like being a sheep without a shepherd. Sheep do not know how to find water and green pasture on their own. Neither do they know how to handle the insects that may get into their wool coats. On their own, they cannot fend off wolves and coyotes, and if they fall, they need assistance with getting back up—much like we need Jesus to help us and save us from the clutches of sin.

My friend, we are living in the last days as described in the Book of Revelation. Time is winding down, and every day that God gives us is a gift—another chance to get it right, especially if we have not accepted Him as our Lord and Savior. Today, if you hear His voice, harden not your heart.

In this "Come to Jesus" moment, He is pulling at the heartstrings of men, women, boys, and girls. He is saying, "Come unto me all ye that labour and are heavy laden, and I will give you rest" (Matthew 11:28).

When my older sister, brother, and I got married to our significant others, our mother and grandfather put their heads together and decided that if we young married people were not going to church, they would bring the church to us. As such, we took turns hosting prayer and worship services in our homes.

The Word of God was made so plain to me during those family sessions. I began to believe in Him, and my faith increased. Jesus became so real to me that when I got up to get the baby her formula early one morning, it seemed like when I turned on the kitchen light, Jesus should have been sitting at the kitchen table. Of course, He wasn't there when I turned on the light. Later that same morning, I was ironing clothes and listening to gospel music on the radio. I listened as someone sang, "Nearer My God to Thee." I began to sing along, and before I knew it, the presence of the Lord came upon me. I did not have to ask anyone what happened; I knew it was the Lord. I know that serving God is a faith walk, but He lets us feel His presence every now and then.

Sometimes, my faith walk has been an uphill journey, and the road has been rocky. I have had to stand still at times and even do my first work over, but God has always been right there by my side. He has never left me alone.

God has never left any of us alone. Many times, we leave Him, but it is not His will that any of us perish.

"The Lord is not slack concerning His promise, as some men count slackness, but is longsuffering to us-ward, not willing that any should perish, but all should come to repentance."
2 Peter 3:9

When I think about what Jesus went through for us—the abuse, the accusations, taking our sins upon Himself when He knew no sin, the beatings, and the blood shed—He still said, "Father, forgive them, for they know not what they do" (Luke 23:34a). We owe Him our lives.

"For as much then as Christ hath suffered for us in the flesh, arm yourselves likewise with the same mind: for He that hath suffered in the flesh hath ceased from sin."
1 Peter 4:1

I am grateful to God that He looked beyond my faults and saw my needs. I found the answer when I learned to pray. God is a God who offers more than a second chance.

"Therefore, my beloved brethren, be ye steadfast, unmovable, always abounding in the work of the Lord; for as much as ye know that your labour is not in vain in the Lord."
1 Corinthians 15:58

Living for Jesus is the right choice. One day, we are going to see Him face to face. What are we going to say then? We want to hear Him say to us, "Come ye blessed of My Father and inherit the kingdom that has been prepared for you from the foundation of the world" (Matthew 2:34).

"For what shall it profit a man if he shall gain the whole world and lose his soul?"
Mark 8:36

The riches of this world last only for a season. We cannot take what we have accumulated in this life with us when we die.

"It is appointed unto man once to die, but after this, the judgment."
Hebrews 9:27

God has given us a way of escape.

"I am the door: by Me, if any man enter in, he shall be saved, and shall go in and out, and find pasture. The thief comes not but for to steal, kill, and destroy; I am come that they may have life and have it more abundantly."
John 10:9-10

If you have accepted Jesus as your Savior, be encouraged. Keep on keeping on for Jesus. Don't be weary in well doing; you shall reap bountiful blessings. If you are reading this and do not have a personal relationship with Jesus, why not give Him a chance to be the Lord and Savior of your life? He is closer to you than the air you are breathing at this very moment.

"That if you confess with your mouth the Lord Jesus and shall believe in your heart that God raised Jesus from the dead, you shall be saved. For with the heart, man believes unto righteousness; and with the mouth, confession is made unto salvation. For the scripture says, 'Whoever believes in Jesus shall not be ashamed.' There is no difference between the Jew and the Greek: for the same Lord over all is rich unto all who call upon Him. For whosoever shall call upon the name of the Lord shall be saved."
Romans 10:9-13

Jesus is the answer for the world today!

Matthew 24 tells about the signs of the end of this age. As we look around, we can see we are living in a time we have never seen before. The Bible says, "Watch, therefore; for ye know not what hour your Lord doth come" (Matthew 24:42).

As it has already been said, Jesus is coming back again. Revelation 1:7 says, "Behold, He cometh with clouds, and every eye shall see Him, and they also which pierced Him: and all kindreds of the earth shall wail because of Him. Even so, Amen."

THE LOST PEACE

I recall attending a Women's Fellowship Conference, and the Guest Speaker's topic was "Lost Piece." The speaker told us about her daughter putting a puzzle together. All of the pieces were there except for one. All corners and outside borders were in place, but there was a missing piece—making the puzzle incomplete. I was inspired and wrote this chapter: "The Lost Peace."

We are sometimes told that our lives are like that puzzle; we have the outside together, but sometimes when we get to the middle of a situation, things are a little mixed up and confusing. Something is missing, which makes our lives incomplete...like that puzzle. The Bible lets me know that God will be all I will allow Him to be to me and even more.

The Lord is always with us. He is a friend who sticks closer than a brother or sister. Before the second marriage, after being with family and friends, the hour would come when it was time to go home. I could not stay with them forever, so when I returned home, I was physically alone.

I was inspired to write "The Lost Peace" after observing someone sitting alone in a vehicle. The thought that came to my mind was, "I wonder what their life is like. Are they happy? Married? Single?" The number one question that crossed my mind was, "Are they a Christian?" Thoughts can take us on a journey—if we choose to follow the lead. That day, I went home and began to write.

I am usually busy, which is a good thing because while I am, I do not think about being home alone. The Lord has promised He will always be with me, and I believe that. He has been and is still with me to this day. I remember desiring someone to be in my life to laugh, talk, cry, shop, take a ride, and sightsee with me. Most importantly, I wanted someone to pray with, grow in the Lord with, and grow old with. Nonetheless, I had no problem eating alone or going to sleep when it was time to retire from a busy day.

Going to church has kept me busy, but no one stays in church all day (except when we have special services). Family members cannot visit all the time, nor would I want them to. All of us need quality time and space. In writing this, I do not think I have ever felt sorry for myself and would not want anyone to feel sorry for me. I feel I am speaking for many single women—and maybe single men—who live alone. We usually have a routine, and most of the time, everything works like clockwork. Still, there are those days when we need someone to be near, but we remember the words that Jesus spoke:

"That men ought always to pray, and not to faint."
Luke 18:1b

The lost peace is not the same for everyone. Our desires are different. Whatever "it" looks like may be important to us but not necessarily so for the next person. Sometimes, I have had mixed emotions and said, "I am glad I do not have someone telling me what to do, what not to do, where to go, and where not to go. I don't have someone complaining about how I spend money, trying to pick my friends, or telling me I am always on the telephone or computer. I don't have to hear about how I don't fix his favorite food like his mother or that I let the gas get too low in the car." The list goes on and on.

I realize I presented a lot of negativities, but that is sometimes how things are in many of our lives. We cannot have our cake and eat it, too—although I think we would like to believe we can.

Because you are not married or there is no one "significant" in your life does not mean your life is incomplete. God the Father, God's Son Jesus, and the power of the Holy Ghost (Holy Spirit) is what makes our lives complete. No human being can do what He does. We must love God and ourselves. We must know who we are and where we are going. Money, houses, land, or worldly things can make us feel complete, but only for a little while. Things get old, and money cannot buy joy, peace, hope, and happiness.

When our spirit man is filled up (or shall I say when it feels like our cup is running over), we are so filled with joy that it makes no difference what the situation may be. We trust God and know He is going to make a way somehow. That is an illustration of completeness. We find the "missing peace" because there is an assurance that everything will be worked out. Praise God! There will be times when you don't feel all bubbly, but down in your sanctified soul, you know it is well and that everything will be all right. There is no feeling of emptiness because the

Holy Spirit comforts us and fills the void. The "Lost Peace" to the puzzle has been found!

We must learn how to encourage ourselves, speak God's Word, and remind Him of His promises. Remember this: An unanswered prayer does not always mean no. Perhaps it's simply not the time for your prayer to be answered.

"No good thing will He withhold from them that walk uprightly."
Psalm 84:11c

As the speaker concluded, she shared with us that they found the missing piece of her daughter's puzzle, and it was complete.

Jesus has the missing pieces to all the puzzles in our lives (some of us have more than one missing piece). God can fill the void in our lives with love, joy, peace, and happiness. Single women and men of God, you do not have to feel alone because Jesus promised never to leave you alone. In fact, He said, "Lo, I am with you always, even unto the end of the world" (Matthew 28:20b).

What are your lost pieces? Finances? The inability to find a much-needed job? Are you unsure about how to manage the money God has already blessed you with? Could it be a lack of peace of mind?

"Thou will keep him in perfect peace, whose mind is stayed on Thee: because he trusted in Thee."
Isaiah 26:3

"Think on those things that are lovely and pure..."
Philippians 4:8

We must seek guidance from the Lord:

"They who seek Him early will find Him."
Proverbs 8:17c

God promised to give us the desires of our hearts in righteousness:

"Delight thyself also in the Lord, and He shall give thee the desires of thine heart."
Psalm 37:4

Until the lost peace in your life is found, keep trusting God and believe His Word. Delight yourself in Him, and He shall give you the desires of your heart.

Since my early teen years (and maybe before then), I felt that being in love was one of the best things that could ever happen in a person's life. I was 19 when I first got married, and from that union, we had three children. I was 52 when my first husband passed away. Afterward, I again felt a void. I "needed" to have someone "significant" in my life.

When I was 73 years old, a nice man came into my life, and we got married. He was a pastor, and I was looking forward to many years of happiness. God allowed us to share one year, three months, and one day of life together before he transitioned from this life to his heavenly reward. God gave me the desires of my heart, even though it was only for a short time. Someone once asked, "If you can trust a puzzle company to make sure every piece is in the box to complete the puzzle, then why can't you trust God that every piece of your life is there for a reason?"

"And we know all things work together for the good to them who love God, to them that are called according to His purpose."
Romans 8:28

God fulfilled my desires to the point that "my hope is built on nothing less than Jesus' blood and righteousness." I am "looking to the hills from whence comes my help; my help comes from the Lord, which made Heaven and earth" (Psalm 121:1-2). God sent His Son to complete my puzzled life. I found the "Lost Peace," for I learned to pray: "When I see Jesus, Amen!"

I am further comforted by Jesus' words, and I pray you are, too:

"Peace I leave with you, my peace I give unto you: not as the world giveth, give I unto you. Let not your heart be troubled, neither let it be afraid."
John 14:27

TOGETHER YET APART: A SAVED WIFE AND AN UNSAVED HUSBAND

"Can two walk together, except they be agreed?"
Amos 3:3

"And the Lord God said, 'It is not good that the man should be alone; I will make him a help mate for him.' And God made woman. Therefore, shall a man leave his father and mother, and shall cleave unto his wife: and they shall be one flesh."
Genesis 2:18,24

Marriage was God's idea. He planned it as the foundation of His earthly kingdom. Many of us who are married or have been married could not wait until we were of age to say, "I do." If we were not saved, we didn't know how to consult God about the matter. We didn't know how to seek the Kingdom of God first for the things we needed in our lives, including a husband or wife. I did not realize I did not have to seek a husband. The Bible clearly states, "He who finds a wife finds a good thing, and obtaineth favor of the Lord" (Proverbs 18:22). Saved women are to stay in their rightful place in God and carry themselves in a respectful and lady-like manner. I would like to think that when most of us women get married, we have hopes and dreams that the marriage will last for a lifetime...but many of us find ourselves trying to survive in a difficult relationship.

The Bible tells a story about Nabal and Abigail, who were husband and wife. Abigail was a woman of good understanding and a beautiful countenance, but Nabal was vulgar, ungrateful, and difficult to get along with. The Bible says he was evil in his doings.

If your husband or wife is not saved, you will likely not see eye-to-eye on many things. When Christ is in a person's life, there should be enough love and trust for each other that will allow the husband and wife to listen to each other, exchange opinions, and feel comfortable in doing so. Again, I remind you: "Can two walk together except they be agreed?" When the Lord is not in your spouse, life sometimes seems like the devil magnifies himself. The enemy can easily get to you by working through the one who is (or should be) closest to you. Who is closer than a husband or wife? When you love your unsaved spouse, and you really want the marriage to work, if it isn't working, it can add stress to your life, which can contribute to many illnesses.

When you are married yet feel apart from your spouse, maybe you can relate to what I am going to say: You attend church and other functions by yourself, with your children, or with other family members and friends. Maybe you isolate yourself or stay home. The list goes on and on. Thank God for those marriages that have been healed. Even though the couple wasn't saved when they got married, they accepted Jesus as Lord and Savior, and now, their marriage is workable, and they can reason together. The Word of God lets us know there is nothing impossible with Him (see Luke 1:37).

The Bible tells us about Saul. He was the king of Israel and of David (the shepherd boy who killed Goliath), who became the harp player for Saul. David was a man of valor, and Saul set him over the men of war. After the slaughter of the Philistine, "Women of all the cities of Israel met King Saul, singing and dancing with tabrets and joy, with instruments of music saying, 'Saul hath slain his thousands and David his ten thousands.'" That displeased Saul very much. From that day forward, Saul had the desire to kill David. When Saul was pursuing David, he and his men were camped near where Nabal's sheep were grazing. David and his men were a protection for the shepherds and sheep. When David and his men were in need of food and provisions, he sent some of his men with a message to Nabal in hopes that he would grant his wish. After all, David and his men had been like a wall around Nabal's sheep.

Nabal's reply was, "Who is this David, and who is the son of Jesse? Do I have to take my bread and my water and my slaughtered meat that I have butchered for my shearers and give it to men of whom I do not even know or from where they are?" Then, one of Nabal's men went to Abigail, the wife of Nabal, and told her what had happened. Abigail, being the understanding and compassionate person she was, made haste and began to gather food and something to drink for David and his men. She gave instructions to Nabal's men, but to her husband, she said nothing.

Abigail and Nabal were together (married, yet apart).

For Abigail to have done that without her husband knowing, she did not want him to become upset and angry. At the time, Nabal was away from home, tending to the sheep in Carmel. After Abigail had taken the food to David, she waited until Nabal was sober and told him what she had done. "Nabal's heart died within him and became as in stone, or he had a stroke and lay paralyzed for about ten days then died" (1 Samuel 25:37).

Sisters and brothers, every saved person wants their marriage to work. There will be times you will not agree, but you do not have to get bent out of shape and fuss or fight. When things seem to go wrong, seek God in prayer. Stand still and see the salvation of the Lord.

When Abigail tried to make conversation with Nabal, I imagine him probably laughing at her, putting her down, and making her feel small and inadequate. One writer said she finally quit trying to talk to him. He went his way, and she went hers. God intervened for Abigail, though. Even with all the negativity, Abigail remained loving and kind.

In some marriages, togetherness never develops. The couple lives together yet apart for the duration. They live as though they are single ("You do your thing, and I'll do mine"). Abigail and Nabal had that kind of marriage. Their values were at opposite extremes. Even though the following scripture had not been recorded at the time, Matthew 6:33a says, "But seek ye first the Kingdom of God, and His righteousness." When it seems like love is over in the marriage, it will help if the focus were on a workable relationship rather than the impossibility of a perfect one. Very few people believe in "the perfect marriage." Regarding Abigail and Nabal, had he been willing to converse or exchange opinions with his wife from the beginning, it's likely their marriage would have been workable.

A pastor once spoke of how he fell into the habit of putting his parishioners above his family without realizing what he was doing. He began to belittle his wife in the presence of others and make decisions for her as though she were a child. His wife smoldered in silence. She wanted him to notice her needs without having to say anything. She even felt selfish for feeling that way. The day arrived when her loneliness was so intense, she had no strength to pretend any longer that everything was all right in the marriage. Her bitterness exploded, causing her to confess her feelings to her husband. "I cannot keep up the face of being a loving pastor's wife any longer," she said.

In the weeks that followed, they had dark days and difficult times, but the pastor's wife's honest confession was the beginning of healing in their marriage. (We must sometimes ask God to open our mate's understanding.) Her husband began to hear her and discovered that his wife was a person who had her own dreams. He encouraged her and helped her pursue those dreams. Along the way, she learned to forgive and love him again. It's imperative that husbands and wives be willing to listen and be a part of each other's interests.

The husband needs the wife to be sensitive and courageous enough to draw him out when he is hurt or confused, even when he is angry and upset. If no one takes the time to listen, how will they know what the other is feeling? A good listener encourages their mate to be him or herself. They let the other talk into their listening ear and refuse to insert observations or criticisms. They give the other the freedom to reveal their whole being and truth. The wife who does that for her husband becomes for him the reflection of God, who wants us to pour out our hearts to Him and find in Him a refuge. The same is true for the husband who does that for his wife.

I can relate to a marriage such as that of Abigail and the pastor's wife. Marriages such as those create loneliness, resentment, confusion, lack of trust, bitterness, discouragement, and so much more. When a Christian is bogged down with any or all of those things, it interferes with one's spiritual growth. It makes a person wish they never said, "I do."

There are times when wives or husbands may have tried to converse with their spouse (as Abigail did), only to receive a negative response or none at all. Then, many times the spouse who is the victim gets out of character and may say, "Later for this! I must be talking to a wall!" or "Can I say or do anything right?" or "What happened? What went wrong?" Many doubts and fear begin to arise, leading to more questions. "Where did I fail?" Maybe you didn't fail at all. Perhaps God was not in the plan.

Think of a time when you met a handsome man or a beautiful woman. They say all the right things. Words flow from their mouth like honey from a honeycomb...until marriage vows are exchanged. We cannot be so naïve to think that everything will be peaches and cream or that we can change a person. Often, there are warning signs that tell us to detour, but we continue driving that "familiar route," only to learn later we have trespassed and gotten on the wrong road. We find ourselves in an unpleasant situation, but we are with the one we chose to be our lawful wedded husband or wife, to have and to hold, until death do us part. It is then we go to great lengths, trying to make the relationship work, only to find ourselves living together, but yet apart.

Don't give up yet! Where there is life, there is hope.

Not every marriage can be saved. You may be forced to leave when physical, mental, or emotional abuse threatens your or your child's safety. Let God direct your prayers. Ask Him to solve the problem His way. Pray that God's will be done. We have that confidence God will work things out according to His will.

Following are some key takeaways:

1. God is still on the throne. He already knows about your problem but put it before Him by praying and fasting.

2. If and when the opportunity presents itself, try to prayerfully converse and exchange opinions with your mate.

3. Open up and make your request known to your spouse as well as God. Women, it is not wise to tell an unsaved husband that:

   a. The husband is to love his wife as Christ loves the church (Ephesians 5:25), although it is true.

   b. Husbands, love your wives and be not bitter against them (Colossians 3:19).

   c. The husband is to live with the wife and honor her, as she is the weaker vessel (1 Peter 3:7).

Those of us who are saved should refrain from negative expressions, especially when an unsaved is sometimes looking for us to stumble and fall. We—the people of God—should let the Lord shine through us and seek the Lord for guidance in what we should speak. Every marriage is different, and spouses know their mate (or at least they should). What works for one may not work for another. We are no longer walking in the flesh but in the spirit.

"'It is not by might or power, but My Spirit,'
saith the Lord of hosts."
Zechariah 4:6b

We must treat our unsaved spouses like any other person. Our job is to lead lost souls to Jesus. Some of the biggest problems faced in any marriage could be spiritual, financial, infidelity, domestic violence, substance abuse, and a multitude of other issues. That should not be with the people of God, but we sometimes find it to be so. It doesn't have to be, though. We can "cast all of our cares and situations on the Lord; He cares for us" (1 Peter 5:7).

The Bible says, "If it be possible, as much as lie in you, live peaceably with all men" (Romans 12:18). We must be loving and kind, conducting ourselves according to God's Word—from the kitchen to the bedroom. The Bible says, "Marriage is honorable and the bed undefiled, but fornication and adulterers, God will judge" (Hebrews 13:4).

I would like to say that after praying, fasting, and crying, my first marriage had a happy ending, but it did not. Out of 29 years of marriage, I was a saved woman for 25 of them. I did not know how to handle poor communication, loneliness, or whatever else was happening. Neither did I know how to give it to God. I separated myself from living with my husband in 1987. Four years later, he passed away. We had resided in the same house but yet were apart. I pray that before he closed his eyes in death, he talked with Jesus and got his life together.

In a marriage, there is an agreement made. Vows have been made that bind both parties together in Holy Matrimony. When that final separation of death came, the feeling of loneliness that I had remained, regardless of our past.

My friend, if you are desiring a spouse, wait on God. The Word tells us not to be "unequally yoked together with unbelievers, for what fellowship have righteousness with unrighteousness? And what communion hath light with darkness?" (2 Corinthians 6:14). If you put Christ first, you will never walk alone.

"When you walk through a storm,
Hold your head up high.
And don't be afraid of the dark;

At the end of the storm is a golden sky
And the sweet silver song of a lark.
Walk on through the wind;
Walk on through the rain.
Though your dreams be tossed and blown,
Walk on...Walk on with hope in your heart,
And you'll never walk alone.
You will never walk alone."

"You Will Never Walk Alone"
By Oscar Hammerstein, II

BEING BLACK AND LIVING IN AMERICA

According to Wikipedia, America is a diverse country racially and ethnically. I am a native of America and have always been proud to be an American, regardless of what has happened in years past and present. After reading history books and National Geographic magazines, and hearing and seeing news from social media, I still say, "God Bless America!"

I was prompted to use the title "Being Black and Living in America" for one of my short stories while watching Channel 6 News one evening. I recall hearing one of the commentators use those exact words.

When I was a child, I thought that people were people. The only difference was the color of our skin because "color was only skin deep." As well, the color of one's skin does not always define their nationality. Many people have the mentality that Black vs. White in America has created hate and war. For just a moment, visualize a group of people who are defined as "Caucasian." Some are Jewish, German, Italian, Irish, Spanish, Southern, etc. Just because they have the same skin color does not mean they want to be stereotyped as being the same. The same applies to a group of people of color. Some are Afro-Americans, Jamaicans, West Indians, Africans, Portuguese, Canadians, etc. We can believe it or not, but GOD created the human race (read Genesis 1:26-28; 2:7). I believe in God's Word. Contrary to popular belief, humans did not derive from animals.

Life has been interesting. The ethnicity of our race has changed throughout the years. We are recognized as Afro-Americans, Black, and, at one time, we were called Negros. God made our race a variety of colors. There are people who are a shade of very dark brown, light brown, tan, coffee, and cream color (so to speak). Some have very fair skin and can pass as being Caucasian if they so desire. Before the COVID pandemic, beaches were crowded with fair-skinned people trying to get a tan. Why is that? I believe it is because Black is beautiful, even if some do not want to admit it. It is puzzling to me because many people look down on people of color like we are less than others, but God made everybody—and He did not make any junk!

When I was young and did not know or understand that I was "fearfully and wonderfully made" (Psalm 139:14), I used to wish that I was another race. I thank God for ministering to me and letting me know that I am somebody just as I am. I am proud to be a Black woman and realize when I am in the eyes of the public, I represent God (which is most important) and Black Christian women.

Being Black and growing up in America, I lived a good life and was well taken care of. In most races of people, there are the saved and unsaved, the wealthy and poor, those who live comfortably and those who do not, and those with good hygiene and those less fortunate. "If we consider ourselves to judge another person, let us judge them by their character and not by the color of their skin" (words spoken by Rev. Dr. Martin Luther King).

I thank God for my family, parents, and grandparents, who are responsible for my existence and upbringing. I am who I am because of the DNA of my parents. We were not rich people but were honest and God-fearing. My father and grandfather worked very hard to care for their family and to help make America great!

Neither of them had a high school education, but they had good morals and mother wit. My mother and grandmother were homemakers. My father mostly worked in factories and also did fieldwork. He was the second oldest of his siblings. At one point, he had to quit school to help care for his younger sisters and brothers. My maternal grandfather stopped attending school in the third grade to help his mother, who did laundry for some of the rich people who lived in the area. He was blessed to purchase property and became a great farmer. The property contained some of the richest soil in the area. He also worked for other farmers and did lawn care for people during the summer months. My oldest brother and I took care of the farm during the day until our grandfather returned home late in the afternoon.

Some of the crops we grew included strawberries, okra, string beans, peppers, tomatoes, watermelons, and cantaloupe. We had a garden that seemed to have anything you could name. We would then take some of the vegetables to a place my grandfather called "The Block." My brother and I peddled produce (tomatoes, lima beans, and corn) to some of the rich people in town.

In my grandparents' home, children did not wake up in the morning and start playing games. We went to work from sunup to sundown. There was always something to do on the farm. We helped plant, hoe, pull weeds, and turn vines so that grandpop could cultivate the crops with the horse and plow. We learned a lot while living on the farm. We picked tomatoes, which we loaded onto the truck to be taken to the canning factory (P.J. Ritters in Bridgeton, New Jersey). I can clearly recall trucks loaded with tomatoes parked on Bowentown Road, West Avenue, and down Broad Street Hill to South Laurel Street, lined up and waiting for their turn to enter the factory. During the tomato season, the smell of ketchup filled the air. We loved that aroma.

We worked so hard from spring to frost that there wasn't much time to think about what was going on in America until school started. I remember having to be quiet in the evenings while grandpop listened to the radio to hear the local and world news.

Our fun winter evening pastime was scooping up snow to make ice cream. We made homemade butter by shaking fresh milk from the dairy farm into a jar until the fat separated. We also made molasses candy. Sometimes, we added walnuts to the molasses. Almost every day, it seemed my grandfather went to the country store for something, and I usually had some pennies to spend. I do not remember the cost of a large bottle of soda, but when we took an empty bottle back to the store, we got a five-cent deposit and a two-cent deposit for each small bottle. We used the refund money as cash to use at the store or took it home to put in our piggy bank. Other fond memories I have are going to the annual County Fair, church outings to Wildwood (the shore), and our family going to Pennsville Amusement Park (if we were on good behavior).

When the weather turned cold, pigs were slaughtered. Some of the meat would be smoked or cured for bacon and ham or salted for fresh port roast or salt pork. Sometimes, the meat was fried and packed into mason jars. The fat was poured over the meat, a lid was applied and tightened, and the jar was inverted until the liquid fat turned solid, which sealed the jar. After the meat was cured, it was hung in the cold cellar on a heavy string. My mother and grandmother canned anything they knew how to can, placing vegetables and preserves into mason jars. We had enough canned vegetables and preserves to last us throughout the winter. Baskets of white potatoes and sweet potatoes were stored for the winter months. In late fall, before the first frost, cabbage and blushed tomatoes were buried in straw on the south side of a building. Oh, what a treat it was to eat Jersey tomatoes in November and December!

God gave my grandfather the wisdom, knowledge, and strength to manage the farm and used its productivity to provide income and survival for the family. I worked very hard on the farm and helped with the housework, but I was never hungry or cold. Even in my youth, I used those times as learning experiences, and they have benefited me in my adult life.

That was how I lived. I was raised a Black girl living in America. I was made to feel like I was a rich Black girl, even though I noticed some of my classmates appeared to have more than I did. Still, I wanted for nothing.

God made us to give Him glory, honor, and praise! He does not care about one's color. The Bible says, "It is He who has made us and not we ourselves; we are His people, and sheep of His pasture" (Psalm 100:3).

"Therefore, all things whatsoever ye would that men should do to you, do ye even so to them; for this is the law and the prophets."
Matthew 7:12

Regardless of color, race, or creed, what God says to one, He says to all. We are to be kind to people, for if we are not, payday is coming after a while.

"Be not deceived. God is not mocked; for whatsoever a man sows, that shall he also reap."
Galatians 6:7

About 70 years ago, we dressed as if we were going to church just to go shopping. When my grandmother spoke to someone while walking down the street, she would say, "How do you do?" If it were a gentleman she spoke to, he would tip his hat. My, how times have changed. If there was a store where the proprietor made it known they did not want to serve us, we would bypass them and go to another store. There were so many stores to patronize, especially convenience stores and sub-shops.

One of the theaters in our town had a balcony. That area was designated for people of color to sit. Was the reason in case there was a fire that persons on the lower level would be more likely to escape without harm? Did the people who made the rules think we were not worth saving? Was it that the people did not want to sit near us because they felt they were better? Only God knows.

What would America look like if there was no janitorial crew to scrub walls and wash windows, not to mention the wisdom and knowledge that God gave the so-called "minority" to birth inventions that would prove to be beneficial as long as there is an America. Wake up, people! Take an honest inventory. If your ways do not align with the Word of God, then you need to pray for revival or salvation. Why? Because America is in a downward spiral, you do not want to be a part of. Yes, many of us have been mistreated, but retaliation does not make things better; it makes them worse. First Lady Michelle Obama is famous for saying, "When they go low, we go high!" Those are words of wisdom. I remember being told that the doctor, grocer, or other people in a high office could be among those who go home after work, dress in ceremonial attire, and attend hate meetings. I thank God that by His grace, we are still here.

Going to school wasn't always fun for me. There would be a particular area on the ride to school where I would get pain in my stomach. I thank God for the friends I had in school, as the good outweighed the bad. To this day, I still have some Caucasian grammar school friends and have met others along the way whom I call friends. Everybody doesn't dislike people of color. The same is in reverse.

I find that there are racist people in all nationalities. I also know that Jesus is the answer for the world today. It has been said the United States of America was founded on biblical principles. That being said, why were Black men castrated, lynched, had their bodies saturated in oil, and roasted over a fire like a pig until their bodies were charred and then dragged through town "for sport"? Children, along with their parents, witnessed those events. That is so sad. When any race of people gets cut, they bleed red, just like everyone else. Jesus said, "This is My commandment, that ye love one another, as I have loved you" (John 15:12). If Black people were considered less than others, why did the White master have sex with Black field workers and nannies and impregnate them? It really doesn't make sense.

God is no respecter of person. It is sad when people misuse others just to get good from them. God made Black people strong, but not to be workhorses. Think about this: Why would a father or mother want a woman of another race (one they consider a minority) to breastfeed their baby? If the surrogate woman had milk in her breasts, she needed the milk for her baby. Even if she had too much milk, why would the master's wife allow the slave woman to be that close to her child to nurture that child internally? In essence, some people want what they want, when they want it, and as long as it appeases them, it is right in their eyes.

Observing justice in the United States of America, it appears there are different laws for different people. Down through the years, I have tried to put a deaf ear to some of Black history because it is saddening. The same is true for Jewish people. The more I am enlightened, I see the Constitution was not designed for people of color. That is why it was so easy for those in authority to function as they did. We must thank God for the Emancipation Proclamation. Even then, some of the White masters did not want to let go of their power. When we do not allow God to be the head of our lives, we are capable of stooping to anything and labeling it as "right." God created this world for everyone to enjoy. Those who reject God's Word will have to one day answer to Him.

The American flag salute says, "I pledge allegiance to the flag of the United States of America, and to the Republic for which it stands, one nation, under God, indivisible, with liberty and justice for all." The reason why the athlete, Colin Kaepernick, knelt and did not salute the American flag was that he was tired of the lies it represented. He was quickly reamed out by some in authority. I believe he was not being disrespectful to the flag or his country; he was being truthful to God and himself.

People have rejected God, and the evils of this world have taken control. That is why Black men are killing each other. Some Caucasians are also killing, stealing, cheating, etc., but it is not publicized anywhere near as much as those of other races of people. A White police officer can put his knee on the neck of a Black man and snuff the life out of him with minimal consequence for his actions. Do you not find it strange that we do not hear of nor see Caucasian young men being shot in the back or witness them lying on the ground, handcuffed and pleading for their lives? Even TV commercials lean toward depicting people of color as poor and degraded when in reality, statistics show Caucasians are the majority in those areas.

On January 6, 2021, if the Commander in Chief had been a man of color and a Black mob had climbed the walls of the Capitol Building and desecrated its interior, the matter would have been handled differently. Everyone—including the President—may have been jailed or shot without explanation and would have been counted as less than citizens of the United States.

Do we believe in God's Word? Are we going to be ready when Jesus comes or sends for us, or will we continue to fight one another because of the color of one's skin or because some people think they are "better than"?

"If a man says that he loves God and hates his brother, he is a liar; for he that loves not his brother, whom he has seen, how can he love God, whom he hath not seen?"
1 John 4:20

One day, I found the answer: I learned to pray. That is how I survive in America as a Black woman. Anyone with a problem associating with someone because of the color of their skin doesn't have to worry about living with them in Heaven.

LET US BIND TOGETHER IN CHRISTIAN LOVE AND COME AGAINST SATAN WITH GOD'S HOLY WORD! STOP FIGHTING ONE ANOTHER!

America has been a country of opportunity. One of my brothers said he has been to many countries, but America is the best he has seen in all his travels. After dropping out of high school, I obtained my GED in my thirties. The Lord then blessed me to get Licensed Practical Nurse training. I passed my boards and was licensed by the State of New Jersey to care for the sick and disabled. At one place of employment, I worked five years as a Nurse's Aide and 22 years as a Nurse. I retired after 27 years of service.

As Black people, we have always had to do more to prove we are somebody. While working as a Charge Nurse, I learned some things while behind closed doors in meetings. I would then try to instill into those who were many times thought less of to stand up, become accountable, and prove that we are somebody. There are far too many who expect us to fail.

If your average is a D, work to increase it to a B. If your average is a B, work to advance to a B+. If your average is an A, move up to an A+. My friend, God is looking for excellence! We are to die daily to the evils of this world and perfect those things that remain.

I imagine Dr. King would shake his head today at all that is happening yet still say, "God bless America! Let freedom ring! We have not reached the mountaintop yet, but don't get weary in well doing, and don't forget the struggles."

It has already been said that many hurts and wrongs have taken place in our nation and the world. The Word of God is the same today as it was yesterday and will be forevermore. The Lord God told Solomon, "If My people, which are called by My name, shall humble themselves and pray and seek My face and turn from their wicked ways, then will I hear from Heaven, and heal their land" (2 Chronicles 7:14). God is still in the forgiving and healing business. The world needs to be healed. We need to be healed as individuals.

"In the weeks, months, years to come,
If God wills it to be so,
Let there be peace on earth, and let it begin with me.
Let us be polite when we are in the marketplace,
Walking on the street wherever we are.
Let us hold open a door, that it does not close in someone's face.
Let us be courteous as we drive our vehicles on the highway.
Let us make ourselves do unto others as we would want them to do unto us.
With the help of the Lord,
Let us treat our neighbor as ourselves.
How do you know? Maybe the person you help today will save your life tomorrow.
But ye brethren, be not weary in well doing."

I pray that all people who do not know Jesus will get to know Him. God is love, and the only way we will love one another and forgive each other in this life is to accept Jesus as the Savior and Lord of our lives. We cannot do this by ourselves. Regardless of what man may think, he is not in charge: God is.

I try to live in harmony with my fellow man because the Word of God says, "Follow peace with all men and holiness without which no man shall see the Lord" (Hebrews 12:14).

HE WHO FINDS A WIFE FINDS A GOOD THING
(Proverbs 18:22)

Reading that scripture clearly shows that a woman does not seek the husband, but the man seeks the wife. That does not excuse the woman from putting her best foot forward, walking with dignity, and presenting herself well.

As young girls, many of us dreamed about a tall, dark, and handsome man—forgetting the qualification for our potential mate is to first have a relationship with Jesus. It's imperative that we yoke with someone who loves the Lord and follows God's leading.

Some people do not have the desire to share their life with anyone. For those who do, we often do not know how to go about it. If we lack wisdom, we are to ask God and not lean unto our own understanding. There are many helpful counselors, such as your pastor and those who are trained professionals, but in all things, we should consult God because He is all-knowing. If He feeds the ravens, makes the flowers grow, and clothes the grass, He will certainly be mindful of the desires and needs of His children. When God created Eve from Adam's rib, her earthly paradise was already prepared for her before she arrived.

"But my God shall supply all your needs according to His riches in glory by Christ Jesus."
Philippians 4:19

Love will last, but there is no longevity in an "only appearance" relationship. Years ago, when I was a teenager, it seemed that some of the guys were looking for someone with a Coca-Cola bottle figure—forgetting that as the years mature, both the male and female body will change in appearance and shape. Even today, some men are looking for a place to hang their hats and obtain aid from some vulnerable woman with a kind heart and an income of her own. Most of us were not born into a wealthy family. We have endured the struggles of life, and some did not wait on the Lord for guidance regarding marital affairs. If we want to be discovered for a lifetime relationship of love and intimacy, we must put first things first. We need to know what the will of the Lord is for our lives, which comes from having a relationship with Jesus. God has given us promises He will keep, but if we are outside of His will and not walking according to His commandments, we will not know His plan for our lives.

In the late 1950s, it was not strange to hear of a couple getting married soon after their 12th-grade graduation. Unlike today's young people, most did not plan to attend college at the time. Many of the young men who lived in rural areas became farmers. Some who lived in town worked in factories. Many young women became housewives. We live in such a modern world today, so much so that if we do not keep up with some of the changes, we will be like a lost person wandering in the forest, not knowing in which direction to go. Down through the years, as I reflected on my life, I should have been into academics at the age of 16 instead of sitting in school daydreaming about being in some guy's arms.

My maternal grandmother was 13 when she got married. Grandpop was nineteen. It was instilled in us that when we came of age, we were expected to get married. Females who were not married were called "old maids" or "spinsters." No one wanted to be called either of those names. So, I got married at the age of nineteen.

I am the mother of three (one son and two daughters), whom I would not trade for anything in the world. I have five grandchildren, six great-grandchildren, five great-great-grandchildren, one daughter-in-law, and an extended family of four stepsons, their wives, and their families.

Even though I was not born into a wealthy family, I still desired the better things in life but did not know how to acquire them. I had not accepted Jesus as my Lord and Savior; therefore, I did not know about seeking God's Kingdom and that all things would be added unto me (read Luke 12:31). Neither did I know that I shall have what I desired when I prayed—if I believed (read Mark 11:24).

Marriage is an everlasting covenant ordained by God between a man and a woman for as long as they both shall live. Sometimes, the vows are broken for whatever reason, but that is not the will of God. The Bible says, "Therefore shall a man leave his father and his mother and shall cleave unto his wife, and they shall be one flesh" (Genesis 2:24). The meaning of cleave is to adhere; to cling to; to be faithful.

A relationship with Jesus has always been essential to maintaining a good marriage, but education and finances are also needed. Marriage is not like pitching a ball. There is no "hit or miss." Instead, there should be a commitment that says, "We are in this together and will make it work somehow with the help of God." A successful marriage involves each mate thinking of the welfare of the other more than themselves.

"Marriage is honorable in all, and the bed undefiled: but whoremongers and adulterers God will judge."
Hebrews 13:4

Many people live together without making a commitment, with the mentality that if the relationship does not work, they can split and go their separate ways. God did not say that a man could go from woman to woman until he found a suitable companion. He said, "...cleave unto his wife [not girlfriend], and they shall be one flesh" (Genesis 2:24).

I come from a large family. While watching my mother cook large quantities of food, I used to say, "I'm not getting married." My aunt would reply, "You should get married if for nothing more than security." That was how it was in the lives of many women. They did not work; they married and depended on their husband.

People get married for one reason or another. Thank God a woman does not have to get married just to survive. Prayerfully, God will send her a soulmate who will love and protect her, and they will have a good life together. Remember: Good looks and sweet words can be very deceiving and are not fertile ground on which to stand for a lifetime.

A godly person expects God to give them a godly companion. Speaking from experience, when things seem out of range in a relationship (not lining up with the Word of God), there are gray flags. Gray flags could be speech, values of life, character, etc.

I'm not judging here, but let me ask: Would you be ashamed to introduce your friend to God face-to-face? If you must stop and think about the answer, most likely, they are not the one for you. We are often so desperate for companionship that we try to "make it work." The Bible says we are to "trust in the Lord with all of our heart and lean not unto our own understanding. In all of our ways, acknowledge Him, and He will direct our path" (Proverbs 3:5-6). When in a relationship, you should not have to pull strings to make it work. Present yourself well and be friendly and respectful.

It is not your job to fix others. No one can fix those things that are not to their liking. We cannot make people be who we would like for them to be. People will be who they are until they want to change or allow God to change them. After all, they may not even see any flaws in their life that need to be fixed!

After exchanging wedding vows, we should prayerfully try to hang in there if we can because we have made a lifetime commitment unto death in the presence of God and usually many witnesses. Now, don't get me wrong: I do not believe there is such a thing as a perfect marriage. We are imperfect people. Even when trying to do everything right, we will mess up somewhere. That is why we must wait on the Lord to send us the proper husband or wife.

I have never understood how two people can be so in love, kind, and respectful to one another before marriage (i.e., opening and holding doors and pulling out chairs), but after the wedding, someone gets amnesia. Harsh words began to flow from the same mouth that once spoke sweet nothings (I am reminded of a wolf dressed in sheep's clothing, looking for its prey). When wedding vows are exchanged, they are to be sealed in cement or iron (so to speak) forever and ever, until death do you part. Wait on God. Let Him direct you to your spouse because He does all things well.

I mentioned "gray flags" before—those things we should notice are a little "off" early on, but we are so involved we do not receive the message clearly. Women, if you have to dress him up because you are ashamed to be seen with him in public, that is a gray flag. If your mate is trying to quit a habit, pray for them and be concerned. If there is a borrowing money issue, is that not a gray flag? A typical conversation has always been more than one person talking. When you cannot get one word in edgewise unless asked a question or if you receive a response that says, "Can we talk about this later?" that is a gray flag moment. Who wants to be married and cannot talk to their spouse "only by appointment"? When there is no prayer life or eagerness to worship together, that's a (you guessed it) gray flag!

I am not being judgmental here. My efforts are to highlight that whatever habits or situations come with a person, they will be evident until they come to themselves and allow God to change them. We must wait on God. We cannot run ahead. We must seek His face. We are reminded in the Bible: "Can two walk together, except they be agreed?" Amos 3:3.

I do not proudly say that I did not take notice of the gray flags in my relationship. Neither did I yield at the stop sign. Much like the prodigal son, I had to come to myself (read Luke 15:17).

About 20 years ago, after my first husband passed, I had the opportunity to get married again. I planned a wedding in 1999 that did not happen. I did not seek God for guidance. I was thinking I would not be alone anymore and would have help paying the utilities. The gentleman was nice and seemed concerned about my welfare, but the God I serve turned all my plans around two weeks before the wedding date.

The pastor (my oldest brother) went into his prayer closet after counseling the groom and me. I did not know about that until the day I called him and said, "Pastor, I have mixed feelings about the wedding."

He replied, "I prayed in my prayer room. I prayed in my office at the church. I prayed until I got a headache. I do not want to show up at the wedding, and I knew I could not ask anyone else." It turned out he had interceded for me, asking God to speak to my heart and get my attention. God heard his prayer. I thank God for my pastor standing in the gap for me. I am sorry for putting him through that stress, all because I tried to do things my way and get ahead of God's plan for my life.

I thought about Saul as he traveled on Damascus Road, breathing out threats against the disciples, when the Lord interrupted his program (read Acts 9). I am so glad God loved me so much that He interrupted my plans. He is a loving Father. There is none like Him!

I felt that God loved me, but after He rescued me from that big mistake I was about to make, I really knew He loved me. God had another plan for me. He could see farther down the road than I ever could. When He showed me those gray flags, I should have yielded to the warnings and stop signs, but I didn't. As a result, I went into depression for a while. I was ashamed of myself because I am a minister of the Gospel. I am supposed to be a light in a dark world and an example to Christian women.

God gave me the strength to get myself together, and I attended church, even though I did not feel like facing the public because of embarrassment. Nonetheless, I knew that I needed strength from the saints of God to make it through. That was not a good position to be in, but through it all, my sisters and brothers in the Lord in my church and neighboring churches showed me so much love.

A lot of hurts could have been avoided had I allowed God to lead me. The divorce rate is so high, even in the church, because many do not take marriage seriously. Listen. God did not create us to do whatever we want to do. He is in charge—always. We are not living in ancient times when men had concubines. No. There is to be one wife to one man. Period.

God had a plan for me. In 2013, He allowed me to marry a man of God—a pastor. Even though the marriage was short-lived, God gave me the desires of my heart.

"For the Lord God is a sun and shield; the Lord will give grace and glory: no good thing will He withhold from them that walk uprightly."
Psalm 84:11

MY NURSING CAREER

When I was a child, I frequently thought about what I wanted to do when I became an adult. It seemed obvious that anyone could be a parent. I thought about being a teacher or secretary. Other times, I considered being a singer and heading to Hollywood. I can never recall saying I wanted to become a nurse. When I went to high school, the curriculum I chose was Bookkeeping. I dropped out of school when I was in 10th grade because I thought I was old enough to make decisions for myself. I couldn't have been more wrong...

I believe my nursing career got its start when I was 13 years old. My mother's sister was a brittle diabetic who loved sweets. Most of the time, she would not adhere to her diet regimen. When her blood sugar level was abnormal, she would be in a confused state or go into a diabetic coma. It was my job to get a urine specimen to see if she needed either insulin or sugar, which was no easy task. While in a coma, she was more dead than alive. If her glucose level was low, we put sugar under her tongue or gave her orange juice (if she could drink it). If her level was elevated, I would give her an insulin injection. No matter the case,

God always led us to do the right thing for her. My aunt taught me how to give her needles by practicing with an orange and needle injector. There was a time when I no longer lived with my aunt and grandparents and there was a problem with her blood sugar; I was summoned.

I got my first job when I was 23 years old as a Nurse's Aide at Cumberland Manor in Bridgeton, New Jersey. At the time, the facility was called "The County Farm."

On the day I applied, I was instructed to leave my name, address, and phone number. I waited for a call from the facility, but none came. I told my neighbor about my disappointment (she was the one who told me about the job), and she said, "You cannot wait for them to call you. You must go back to them." I did as she said—and was hired on the spot! I was told there was an emergency that needed immediate tending to. When I heard the word "emergency," I thought to myself, "They must be doing surgery." I knew nothing about nursing homes (a.k.a. the old folks' home). Sometimes, my family members went to the hospital if they had some kind of illness that home remedies couldn't resolve, but none had been in a nursing home.

The charge nurse took me to the floor where help was needed. She said, "You take care of the elderly like you would take care of your children." I was surprised and shocked to see older people who were wrinkled with flabby skin. Some were so thin, they looked like skin and bones. My parents and grandparents did not make a habit of walking around without wearing clothes, so I had never seen anything like it.

I returned to work the next day. I learned I liked caring for the elderly. I worked for six months but had to quit because of babysitter problems.

Years later, I got a job at another geriatric facility. Even though I felt that caring for the elderly was a great responsibility, I needed money to help make ends meet. With some experience under my belt, I had no problem getting a job.

At the age of 30, I returned to The County Farm. By then, it had been renamed Cumberland Manor. I was hired to work the midnight shift (12 a.m. to 8 a.m.). During the day, I attended a 13-week Nurse's Aide program. I was one of the most achieved students with the highest grades.

After the training, I continued working at Cumberland Manor. I thought I was satisfied with working in that capacity until one morning, just before the break of dawn, I decided I could do better and pursued higher learning in the medical field.

I had been out of school for a few years and realized that even though I had obtained a High School Equivalent Diploma, by dropping out of high school, I had missed out on a lot of academic studies. Therefore, I decided to seek out a Practical Nurse program instead of going to school to become a Registered Nurse.

In September 1976, I enrolled in an 18-month nursing program at Millville Senior High School. The preclinical studies were two-and-a-quarter hours a day and ended in June. Along the way, I received much encouragement from my mother, other family members, and friends. We were allowed to wear street clothes in our preclinical studies. To save money, I got the sewing machine out and made my clothes for class. I also worked 40 hours a week in the evening while in training.

As you can see, I had a full schedule. I was told by those who had already made the grade, "Do not look at the 18 months of training; take one day at a time." Doing just that worked! The scripture that got me through was, "I can do all things through Christ who strengthens me" (Philippians 4:13).

Summer vacation was very short that year. I started clinical training a few days after the 4th of July holiday. The first clinical studies were at Ancora State Psychiatric Hospital. Then we went to Bridgeton Hospital for Pediatrics, then to Med Surge, Obstetrics, etc. What a challenge! Following those studies, I was assigned to the operating room for observation of the removal of a kidney (nephrectomy), removal of a gall bladder (cholecystectomy), a hip replacement, upper GI Series (studies of the gastric system), and colonoscopies. In obstetrics, we trained in the labor room, delivery room, nursery, and postpartum care. There was so much to see and do. I cannot tell it all, but what an experience it was!

One of the most interesting mornings was in the morgue, observing an autopsy. We were instructed to refer to the body as "Mr." Had it been a female, we would have said "Miss" or "Mrs." Can you imagine still having an appetite for lunch after seeing the pathologist cut away body tissue for clinical studies? Believe it or not, we did.

Many times, I wanted to quit the program. It was not easy being introduced to a new subject on a Monday and having to be prepared for a test on Friday. One day, it seemed the Preclinical Instructor was trying to weed out the weaker ones in the class by giving us a pop quiz. I thank God for prompting me the night before to study. I passed the test. I worked and went to school until four months before graduation, which was on March 15th, 1978.

Sometimes, the task that is set before us seems so hard, and we don't think we can make it. We cannot do it by ourselves. Our faith in God will give us that needed push, strength, and hope.

"Nay, in all these things, we are more than conquerors through Him that loved us."
Romans 8:37

I know it was God who made the way and got me through. I had a young child who really needed me by her side—although she seemed very grown up, which made my studying easier. It was such a blessing to have my oldest daughter available to babysit her little sister. I cannot fail to mention my mother as well. She was always in my corner. While in training on my birthday, she cooked a big dinner and invited my sisters, brothers, some of my aunts, friends, and other family members to come for the celebration and blessed me with monetary gifts to assist with some of my expenses. My parents seemed very proud to say, "My daughter is a nurse!"

After graduation, I applied to Cumberland Manor for employment. I heard that the Director of Nurses had no intention of hiring me. Therefore, I also applied for jobs at other facilities. I later received a telephone call from the Director of Nursing at Cumberland Manor, wanting to know if I was still interested in working there. Of course, I was interested! I was familiar with the facility and the way things were done, and I knew most of the residents and employees.

Finally, the day came for the interview. During the interview, the Director asked, "If I give you an assignment, will you be able to carry it out?" I replied, "Yes." As she continued, she stated, "Don't get pregnant. You will be taking your Boards in April. If you fail, you must go back to school for a refresher course and will have to take your Boards over again." She really sounded like she did not want to hire me, right? She was not encouraging at all.

Being a charge nurse over some of the people I had previously worked with side-by-side was not an easy transition. I was told to gain respect from the nurse's aides and that they were not allowed to call me by my first name. Most of the staff were very friendly and congratulated me on my achievements. There was one, however, who did not bite her tongue when she told me she was not going to change a thing—but God worked that out. The God I serve sits high and looks very low. He sees all things and is concerned about His children. Sometimes, he touches the hearts and minds of others and makes them do the very opposite of their intentions.

When the time came, I went to Atlantic City to take my Boards. I traveled home feeling very victorious. To God be the glory! A few weeks later, I went to the mailbox, and there were my results: I had passed!

After becoming a nurse and sitting in meetings, it appeared that Afro-Americans were expected to fail and that they were incapable of pursuing excellence. That is sad. Once in a position of leadership, I wanted every Nurse's Aide whom I gave an assignment to do the very best according to their ability. I told those of color that their work must be above average. I tried to instill in them that we are somebody as individuals, not a race of stereotypical people. The same applies to most people who are taking responsibility for their lives with the help of God, regardless of their nationality.

Well, a new phase had begun in my life. I was proud of the accomplishment. Plus, the training had been beneficial in my personal life and the lives of others. When I was fresh out of school, family members would ask questions about medications and physical ailments. I knew some things, but I referred them to their physician instead.

When I graduated from nursing school, I was 38 years old. Over time, many things have changed, especially since COVID-19. Today, we live in a changing world, but God never changes. "He is the same yesterday, today, and forever" (Hebrews 13:8).

While employed at Cumberland Manor, I worked every shift as a Nurse's Aide and Nurse. Cumberland Manor was a beautiful facility. It was clean, the care was excellent, and the Director of Nursing ordered the best medical supplies on the market at the time. We did not use generic products for our patients' treatments. In the '70s and '80s, we had a good security staff, the cleaning crew was efficient, the kitchen staff was superb, and caring people were working in the laundry. We were like family. Cumberland Manor was the place to work and provided good benefits, including sick days, holidays, personal days, bereavement days, and vacation days.

Cumberland Manor was a 190-plus-bed facility with three floors. Working as a charge nurse, I could see the benefit of having at least eight Nurse's Aides on each floor during the day shift to help meet the residents' needs. Some of my duties as a charge nurse included receiving the outgoing nurses' floor reports and giving them to the oncoming shift, along with assigning the Certified Nursing Assistants their duties. I also made phone calls to doctors and families and took care of death and dying procedures. Whatever happened on the floor that I was assigned to, it was my job to ensure things ran smoothly. I thank God for the ward clerk. She was such a blessing. So much can be said about nursing, but at the end of the day, it requires a staff that can work together as a team to get the job done.

When I graduated from LPN school, my uniform consisted of a white dress, white shoes, and a white nurse's cap with gold wings on a black velvet ribbon that was attached to my cap. I was so proud of my cap because I had worked very hard to earn it. According to Wikipedia, "By the 1980s, nurses' caps all but disappeared with the universal adoption of scrubs." Many times, when you walk into a hospital or nursing facility nowadays, it's rare to be able to easily distinguish between a nurse and a nursing assistant.

It seemed by being a Black nurse, I had to excel in my job performance and work ethic. "Fair" or a B grade was not good enough; I had to strive for an A or A+. I had to make a difference. In all of my trying to do things right, I made mistakes. There were those who tried to count me out, but God! God gets the glory, the honor, and the praise! I could not have done it by myself. I proudly would try to accomplish the daily tasks set before me with my head up, shoulders back, and my face to the wind.

"I will lift up mine eyes unto the hills from whence comes my help; my help comes from the Lord which made Heaven and earth."
Psalm 121:1-2

A few of the recognitions and awards I received during my career were:

- 1977 – I received a Five-Year Nurse's Aide Service Award from the Board of Freeholders of Cumberland County, New Jersey.
- 1978 – I received a Letter of Recognition of Congratulations regarding my nursing career.
- 1979 – I received a Perfect Attendance Award.
- 1985 – I received an Employee of the Month Award, where I was recognized for excellent bedside nursing skills as a Nurse's Aide before becoming a Nurse, and as a Nurse for consistently performing required nursing duties, completing treatments, giving medications, charting, and direct patient care.
- 1993 – I received a Certificate of Excellence in Nursing.
- 1996 – I received the Bronze Star Award that was sponsored by The African- American Women's

Network at the Hilton Hotel in Cherry Hill, New Jersey.

Today, I encourage every man, woman, boy, and girl not to feel intimidated by those who try to appear superior to them. I tell them, "If God is for you, He is more than the whole world against you! What God has for you is for you."

I retired from Cumberland Manor in 2000. I felt I needed a few extra dollars to supplement my income, so I pursued a part-time job. Nursing is not an easy vocation, but being a nurse is what I knew to do best. One of my friends, a supervisor in a Mental Health Unit, told me about their need for a Licensed Practical Nurse on the midnight shift (it's nice to have friends in high places). I worked there until I fell ill and had to stop working. It was actually one of the easiest jobs I've had, paid the most for the number of hours I worked, and was the most dangerous job I ever had—although I only worked four days a month.

Regardless of your career path—whether white collar, blue collar, housekeeper, street sweeper, dishwasher, burger flipper, cashier, preacher, teacher, or whatever it may be—be the very best you can be. Yes, you may encounter days when you are discouraged. Not all employers treat their employees fairly but remember that God is taking inventory of all that is happening. He is always mindful of you, and He cares.

"The eyes of the Lord are upon the righteous, and His ears are open unto their cry."
Psalm 34:15

You are further encouraged to memorize and allow the following scripture to get you through challenging situations:

"I can do all things through Christ who strengthens me."
Philippians 4:13

May God continue to bless you. He is not through with you yet. Believe it; receive it!

WHO IS YOUR BEST FRIEND?

"A friend loves at all times..."
Proverbs 17:17a

Afriend loves in good times and when times do not seem to be good. A friend will not leave you standing alone. There is no friend like Jesus. He knows all about our struggles and will stick closer than a sister or brother. Someone said, "I searched all over but couldn't find nobody greater than Jesus." Amen to that!

When I was a child, I had one special friend to whom I could tell all my secrets and vice versa. The one telling the secret would say, "I will tell you a secret, but you can't tell anybody. You gotta promise." The reply would be, "I won't tell anybody. I cross my heart and hope to die." (Did we really know what we were saying? I hope to die. No!) We were anxious to hear each other's secrets, which were things we would not want our parents or anyone else to know. A secret was to be kept hidden. No one was supposed to know outside of the two of us...friends.

We did not realize at the time that our secrets were words spoken that should not have been said, or we were listening to junk that should not have entered our ears. Believe it or not, back in the day, if we said something that our mother or grandmother deemed unfit to come out of our mouths, we might get our mouths washed with soap or have black pepper put on our tongues. Our parents loved us; they told us so. They wanted us to do the right thing, even if they thought they had to scare doing right into us.

Later, one of us would hear that someone else knows the secret. That was when we realized: I was not the only best friend. The supposed-to-be best friend had another friend, and friends tell other friends secrets. Even though we vowed never to tell another, that promise had been broken, and personal information shared in confidence has been broadcast. Enter feelings of hurt, shame, embarrassment, desertion, rejection, and abandonment. It is now known that the best friend was not a "bestie" after all.

We used to play a game called "The Farmer in the Dell." We would hold hands and form a circle. One person was chosen to be the farmer and would go to the circle's center. The children would walk around the farmer singing, "The farmer in the dell; hi-ho the derry-o; the farmer in the dell." From the circle of children, the farmer chose a wife, the wife chose a child, the child chose a nurse, the nurse chose a cow, the cow chose a dog, the dog chose a cat, the cat chose a rat, and the rat took the cheese. The cheese had no one to choose from, so at the conclusion of the game, the cheese stood alone. Although the game stems from a nursery rhyme, being left alone did not feel good. Of course, we know that cheese does not stand alone, as it is a delicious dairy product many of us enjoy eating.

The following hymn has been a blessing to me throughout the years. Many times, when I have felt rejected or alone, Jesus has always been there to pick me up with a spoken Word of God—either read or sung. Prayerfully read the words and let them minister to you.

"There's Not a Friend Like the Lowly Jesus"
by Johnson Oatman (1895)

1. There's not a friend like the lowly Jesus. No, not one. None else can heal all our soul's diseases. No, not one.
2. No friend like Him is so high and holy. No, not one. And yet no friend is so meek and lowly.No, not one.

3. There's not an hour that He is not near us. No, not one. No night so dark, but His love can cheer us. No, not one.

4. Did ever saints find this Friend forsake him? No, not one. Or sinner find that He would not take him? No, not one.

5. Was e'er a gift, like the Savior, given? No, not one. Will He refuse us a home in Heaven? No, not one.

Chorus:

Jesus knows all about our struggles. He will guide till the day is done. There's not a friend like the lowly Jesus. No, not one; no, not one!

I believe that many of us would like to feel that we belong—that we are associated with a group—especially with the family of God. We want to feel that we fit in somewhere. Sometimes, we allow the enemy to make us think that no one loves or cares about us. If family and friends have left you alone, like the songwriter said, "There's not a friend like Jesus." He is with you now. When you depart from this life, He will be there to welcome you into Heaven. Family and friends can only go as far as the grave. Many times, some soon forget what matter of person you were.

There is no place on this earth we can go and get away from the presence of the Lord. In Psalm 139:7-12, the Psalmist wrote, "Whither shall I go from thy Spirit? Or whither shall I flee from Thy presence? If I ascend up into Heaven, Thou art there: if I make my bed in Hell, Thou art there. If I take the wings of the morning and dwell in the uttermost parts of the sea, even there shall Thy hand lead me, and Thy right hand shall hold me. If I say surely the darkness shall cover me, even the night shall be light about me. Yea, the darkness hides not from Thee, but the night shines as the day. The darkness and the light are both alike to Thee."

God is Omnipresent (He is everywhere).
God is Omniscient (He is all-knowing).
God is Omnipotent (He is all power).
God is Immutable (He never changes).

Family and friends may change on us, many times because they forgot their promise. Perhaps a problem arose, and the promise could not be carried out. Maybe they simply didn't care. No matter the case, a child of God can never move beyond His care, guidance, and supporting strength as long as they abide in God's Word. Whatever the present and future hold, God will be with us in all troubles.

"Trust ye not in a friend;
put ye not confidence in a guide."
Micah 7:5a-b

"But my God shall supply all your needs, according to
His riches in glory by Christ Jesus."
Philippians 4:19

"I will lift mine eyes unto the hills from whence comes
my help; my help comes from the Lord, which made
Heaven and earth."
Psalm 121:1-2

We can tell Jesus what is in our hearts and on our minds. Even though He already knows, He will never tell another. By His Word, our steps are ordered. Take some time to tell him what's on your mind. He is the lifter of your head. He will wipe the tears from your eyes and turn your midnight into day. Just a reminder: Jesus is a Friend who will stick closer than a brother or sister.

The greatest need is for us to know who Jesus is and accept Him as Lord and Savior. While in this life, He can and will fix your "it" if you let him, whether spiritual, physical, psychological, financial, marital or whatever the case may be. When I was a young Christian, I wish I had known then what I know now. I surely would have done things so much differently. Many times, I would tell someone (whoever would listen) my troubles, hoping they would not tell anyone. At the end of the day, I always told Jesus. No one else could solve my problems because they couldn't even solve their own. I should have done like the Apostle Paul said in 1 Peter 5:7: "Casting all your care upon Him, for He cares for you."

God is concerned about us. He will teach, lead, and guide us. Your life is an open book before God, for He knows, sees, and cares about you. When your life seems upside down, and you feel alone, there will never be a friend like Jesus.

I find that I can tell Jesus any and everything. He will share my burdens and bear them. I do not need a group or a cheer team because my strength, hope, ambition, and encouragement lie in Him. Jesus said, "Ye are my friends, if ye do whatsoever I command you" (John 15:14). He is the best of all friends. He never sleeps nor slumbers. He is always watching over us.

Live for Jesus. That is what matters. Be thankful. Be holy. Pray and read your bible daily. Within, you will find life and help along the way. Keep trusting, and don't give up on God because He will never give up on you. He is able to do all that He has promised He would do.

Now, unto Him who is able to do exceedingly abundantly above all that we ask or think, according to the power that worketh in us, unto Him be glory in the church by Christ Jesus throughout all ages, world without end. Amen.

God Bless You!

THE CONCLUSION OF THE WHOLE MATTER

I pray that as you read the stories, something written encouraged you. If only one point spoke to your spirit, it was worth my time and effort. I desire to help others as I journey through this land with life's trials, singing as I go. Most importantly, I desire to point someone's soul to Calvary.

I thank God for my cousin, Marlowe R. Scott, for her encouragement to write, and her daughter, Angela R. Edwards, the CEO and Chief Editorial Director of Pearly Gates Publishing, LLC. For years, I wondered who would publish a book if I wrote one.

"There is no secret to what God can do!
What He's done for others, He can do for you!"

With the help of God, Marlowe, and Angela, I wrote a contributory short story called "When Midnight Strikes at 3:37 P.M." in a book titled "God Says I am Battle-Scar Free: Testimonies of Abuse Survivors – Part Two, compiled by Angela R. Edwards.

I have also contributed original poetry to the following projects:

- "My Special Cousin" in "Poetic Pearls & Gems with Purpose"—a collaboration by Angela R. Edwards.
- "If You Only Knew Who I Am" in "Poetic Voices: Seeking Solidarity During Racial Transitions"—a collaboration by Angela R. Edwards and Marlowe R. Scott.
- "For All He Has Done" in "Pentecost: Where the Spirit of God Is" by #1 Bestselling International Author Marlowe R. Scott.

Jesus is the answer for the world today, my friend! God Bless You!

"Behold, I come quickly: blessed is he that keeps the sayings of the prophecy of this book."
Revelation 22:7

Jesus Is Coming Soon!

ABOUT THE AUTHOR

Arlene Holden was born in Bridgeton, New Jersey, in Cumberland County, on September 11, 1939, to the late James C. and Pearl F. Pernell. She is one of 13 siblings. At the time of this publication, seven are deceased.

Arlene is a widow, a mother of three, a grandmother, a great-grandmother, and a great-great-grandmother. She married Elvin Powell, Jr. on March 23, 1958. Twenty-two years after his demise, she married Elder Harmon Holden, who is also deceased.

Arlene is a retired nurse. Previous employment included domestic work, a school bus driver, and life as a homemaker. Most importantly, she accepted Jesus as her personal Lord and Savior. In the early 1980s, she heard and heeded the call to ministry.

Arlene states, "I have found that I can live today and face tomorrow because Jesus lives! He lives within my heart!"